THE POETRY OF
DOROTHY WORDSWORTH

ẽ ẽ ẽ The Poetry of Dorothy Wordsworth

EDITED FROM THE JOURNALS

BY HYMAN EIGERMAN

GREENWOOD PRESS, PUBLISHERS
WESTPORT, CONNECTICUT

To
Leah and Daniel

FOREWORD

FOR years I have been telling my classes that it is a pity
to regard the journals of Dorothy Wordsworth merely as
a mass of footnotes to her brother's poems, that she de-
serves to be regarded as a poet in her own right. Quite
independently, Mr. Eigerman has arrived at the same
opinion, but he has driven the point home in a way which
had never occurred to me. He has selected representative
passages from the journals and with a skill which does
credit to his own poetic sensibility has arranged them in
lines of free verse.

The scholar who may be inclined to frown at this
rather violent treatment of a respected document of the
romantic period is invited to suspend judgment until he
has considered the result. The device, it seems to me, has
added a new and very interesting figure to the company
of English poets. No one would assert that Dorothy is a
sublime, neglected genius; she is not for a moment to be
compared with the great romantics. But among the minor
poets of the period, I do not know a keener or more lov-
ing eye, a more responsive heart, a gentler, purer, truer
utterance than hers. It is well to have her poetry sifted
out and presented to us in a form which properly em-

phasizes its images and cadences. "Her voice was like a hidden bird that sang," wrote William in the *Recluse* fragment. I hope this voice will now be heard by many.

For the sake of Dorothy's fame, I could wish that Mr. Eigerman had done her this good turn about twenty years ago. She is not in the least like Keats or like Spender, but she is amazingly like the best of those Imagist poets who have now become somewhat difficult to recall. To avoid the feeling that she is pleasantly old-fashioned, let us remember her dates; she will then seem quite startling in her modernity. Immediate sensuous experience observed with breathless intentness and set down in words of simple accuracy which move to a purely organic rhythm; total absence of self-conscious eloquence; delicate unexplicit suggestion, largely through the objective material itself, of emotional and conceptual response—this is what, at her best, she has to give, and we must pass onward for nearly a century before we find the same combination of qualities in English poetry. That she never dreamed that she was writing poetry in her journals adds to the piquancy of the situation and raises interesting historical and critical questions.

"She gave me eyes, she gave me ears." More clearly than before, after reading these poems, we understand her brother's tribute. Dorothy did not rival William in artistry, or imaginative power, or passionate wisdom; but she possessed as fully as he, and with less admixture of didacticism, that sensuousness which is the basis of all poetry and which he himself lost too soon. As the visionary gleam faded, there were times when he envied a little the gypsy freshness and immediacy of Dorothy's communion with the spirit of nature. Hence, in "Tintern Abbey," after one of his most eloquent attempts to persuade himself that the philosophy of nature is an adequate compensation for the loss of childhood's simpler vision, he turns to her with the cry:

> Oh! yet a little while
> May I behold in thee what I was once,
> My dear, dear Sister! And this prayer I make,
> Knowing that Nature never did betray
> The heart that loved her;
>
> . . . .
>
> Therefore let the moon
> Shine on thee in thy solitary walk;
> And let the misty mountain winds be free
> To blow against thee:

A little smugly he prophesies the coming of a time

> When these wild ecstasies shall be matured
> Into a sober pleasure,

but he reflects that when she has achieved wisdom he himself may be

> where I no more can hear
> Thy voice, nor catch from thy wild eyes these gleams
> Of past existence.

These pages contain the winnowed harvest of her walks.

H. N. F.

Hunter College of the City of New York
August, 1940

PREFACE

THE following pieces were written by Dorothy Words-
worth. They were written across the page—without open
recognition of their character as poems. That Dorothy
had at least a strong suspicion, though a baffled one, of
the poetic character of her observations may be inferred
from the passage, in Number 27, in which she writes of
one scene of natural beauty that it has made her "more
than half a poet." I think it is not only permissible but
obligatory that scholars who come after the Imagists and
free verse should do their duty as the literary executors
of the past and resolve for Dorothy Wordsworth that
dilemma which is stated when we couple the above
quotation with her other journal jotting: "I tried to write
verses—alas!" This executorship I have tried to fulfill by
lifting out of the context those passages of her journals
which have seemed to me to rise into poetry, preserving
the words and the word order of the original, only mar-
shaling them within the free-verse form which was un-
known to their author.

This process of selection and the new line divisions
given to the passages selected—both of which operations
are closely governed by the original text and so by its

author—are all that the work of editorship has involved in the case of seventy of the eighty-four pieces which make up this volume. The remaining fourteen selections have been subjected to further manipulations which have seemed to me to be quite justifiable. If any reader feel, however, that too much has been done to some or all of these fourteen to permit them to be regarded as poems written by Dorothy Wordsworth, it is to be hoped that the other five-sixths of the book will already have established her as an English poet.

The last sixth may be divided into several groups. In the first group may be placed three poems—Numbers 51, 61, and 70. Both stanzas in each of these pieces are taken from the same narrative or descriptive passage in the journals. But the original text also had some eight lines of prose between what are now the two stanzas, lines which were regarded as either too prosy or productive of too heterogeneous a whole. To put into somewhat closer association two poetic passages which are already associated in the original will not, I hope, be deemed too violent an operation on the text. Concerning the lovely poem on Calais beach—Number 51—the most important of these three, it should be remembered that at worst the two stanzas may still be read very effectively as separate pieces, though that effort will itself point the fact that they belong together and thus justify joining them.

Number 43 has required another type of special treatment. In the original some rather commonplace remarks about the columbine are followed by an interesting poetical statement. The subject of the poetic observation has been stated some two lines back and, naturally, is not repeated. In this book, the subject has been joined to its poetic predicate, and we read: "The columbine is a graceful slender creature." Numbers 10 and 37 have the same sort of statement of the subject in the first line, omitting the three lines which in the original separate it from the main body of the poem.

The remaining eight of these fourteen pieces—Numbers 5, 19, 40, 44, 45, 52, 53, and 68—each have had a single word or phrase removed. In some cases, the word or phrase is there only because of the position of the passage in the context. As soon as it is lifted from the context, the word or phrase becomes irrelevant. So, in the case of Number 52, the original reads: "It was also beautiful." The word *also* appears in the original because this passage is preceded by a list of other beautiful things. If the passage had been presented without the context, there can be little question that the author would have struck out the word *also*. Similarly, Numbers 40 and 68 have been pruned of a phrase devoted to carrying on the larger narrative of the context. The other five pieces have each suffered excision of a marring word or phrase on the theory that if any formal presentation of the passage had later been undertaken by the writer, she would have been certain to strike out the careless word or phrase. For example, in Number 5 the original text reads: "hanging, as it were, in one undetermined line." The words *as it were* have been cut out of the present version. On the same grounds, a similar operation was performed in Numbers 19, 44, 45, and 53. It should, however, be pointed out that in Number 19 the offending words amounted to a short sentence. After the fourth line of the present version, the original has the unhappy observation that "Her father lived to the age of 105."

The task of compiling this little book has been a very enjoyable one, and in the course of it I have had the pleasure of acquiring numerous debts for assistance and criticism. I should like to acknowledge here at least those which were not purely personal but had some direct effect on the text.

Professor Hoxie Neale Fairchild, who acted as sponsor and godfather to this volume, also read the manuscript and generously gave valuable advice on some of the main general policies governing the making of the book and on a number of specific questions in the editing of individual pieces.

I had the helpful assistance and criticism of my wife, Leah Eigerman, at every point in the editing of this book. Many a knot was cut by her forceful directness, and several of the pieces in this volume are of her discovery or salvaging.

To Miss Evelyn Gordon, to Dr. Irene Jaworski, and to Mr. Arne Gronningsater, I am indebted for criticism of considerable portions of the manuscript.

H. E.

New York
August, 1940

ACKNOWLEDGMENT

THE editor wishes to acknowledge the permission granted him by Macmillan & Co., Ltd., of London and The Macmillan Company of New York to use these selections, taken in the following order from the *Journals of Dorothy Wordsworth*, edited by William Knight, London, 1930, pages 3, 3-4, 7, 7, 9, 11, 11, 11-12, 12-13, 17, 32, 43, 56, 57, 64-65, 73, 83, 85, 90, 90-91, 97, 98, 101, 101, 102, 102, 102, 103, 105, 105, 106, 108-9, 109, 109, 112, 112, 115, 116, 116, 116-17, 121, 124, 125, 126, 131, 132, 132, 133, 134, 137, 146-47, 147, 150-51, 153, 155, 157, 163, 164, 165, 171, 175, 186, 190, 207, 212-13, 256, 268, 303-4, 306, 366, 393, 394, 405, 405, 444, 449, 457-58, 463, 483, 496, 501, 519, 536, 536.

CONTENTS

ALFOXDEN

(1798)

1

The green paths down the hill-sides
Are channels for streams;
The young wheat is streaked
By silver lines of water
Running between the ridges;
The sheep are gathered together on the slopes.

After the wet dark days
The country seems more populous.
It peoples itself in the sunbeams.
The garden, mimic of Spring,
Is gay with flowers.
The purple-starred hepatica
Spreads itself in the sun,
And the clustering snow-drops
Put forth their white heads,
At first, upright, ribbed with green,
And like a rosebud when completely opened,
Hanging their heads downwards,
But slowly lengthening their slender stems.

The slanting woods of an unvarying brown,
Showing the light
Through the thin net-work of their upper boughs.

Upon the highest ridge of that round hill
Covered with planted oaks
The shafts of the trees show in the light
Like the columns of a ruin.

〰. 2

Through the wood to Holford—
The ivy twisting round the oaks
Like bristled serpents.
The day cold—
A warm shelter in the hollies
Capriciously bearing berries.

Query: Are the male and female flowers
On separate trees?

᠗ 3

Young lambs
In a green pasture in the Coombe—
Thick legs,
Large heads,
Black staring eyes.

4

Gathered sticks in the wood;
A perfect stillness.
The redbreasts sang
Upon the leafless boughs.

5

The ridges of the hills
Fringed with wood,
Showing the sea through them
Like the white sky,
And still beyond
The dim horizon of the distant hills,
Hanging
In one undetermined line
Between sea and sky.

流. 6

A winter prospect
Shows
Every cottage
Every farm
And the forms of distant trees.

7

While the twilight
Still overpowered the light of the moon,
We were reminded
That she was shining
Bright above our heads,
By our faint shadows going before us.
We had seen her
On the tops of the hills,
Melting into the blue sky.

ཧ. 8

Venus,
Almost like another moon,
Lost to us at Alfoxden
Long before
She goes down the large white sea.

茶. 9

One only leaf
Upon the top of a tree—
The sole remaining leaf—
Danced round and round
Like a rag
Blown by the wind.

🕊 10

Walked about the squire's grounds:
The dell romantic and beautiful
Though everywhere planted
With unnaturalized trees.

Happily,
We cannot shape out the huge hills
Or carve out the valleys.

GRASMERE

(1800-1803)

徊. 11

Grasmere very solemn
In the last glimpse of twilight.
It calls home the heart
To quietness.

笭 12

We saw a raven very high above us.
It called out, and the dome of the sky
Seemed to echo the sound.
It called again and again as it flew onwards,
And the mountains gave back the sound
Seeming as if from their centre—
A musical bell-like answering
To the bird's hoarse voice.
We heard both the call of the bird
And the echo
After we could see him no longer.

ঌ. 13

The moon shone
Like herrings in the water.

꼰. 14

The hills,
And the stars,
And the white waters
With their ever varying,
Yet ceaseless sound.

〰 15

We stood there a long time,
The whole scene impressive.
The mountains indistinct,
The Lake calm and partly ruffled.
A sweet sound of water falling
Into the quiet Lake.

A storm was gathering in Easedale,
So we returned;
But the moon came out,
And opened to us
The church and village.

Helm Crag in shade,
The larger mountains dappled like a sky.
We stood long upon the bridge,
Wished for William.

๑ 16

We overtook old Fleming at Rydale,
Leading his little Dutchman-like grandchild
Along the slippery road.
The same pace
Seemed to be natural to them both—
The old man and the little child—
And they went hand in hand,
The grandfather cautious,
Yet looking proud of his charge.

17

There was an unusual softness
In the prospects, as we went,
A rich yellow upon the fields,
And a soft grave purple on the waters.
When we returned many stars were out,
The clouds were moveless,
In the sky, soft purple,
The lake of Rydale calm, Jupiter behind.
Jupiter at least *we* call him, but William says
We always call the brightest star Jupiter.

18

I found a strawberry blossom in a rock.
The little slender flower had more courage
Than the green leaves,
For *they* were but half expanded, and half grown,
But the blossom was spread full out.

19

A poor woman came, she said,
To beg.
But she has been used to go a-begging,
For she has often come here.
She is a woman of strong bones
With a complexion that has been beautiful
And remained very fresh last year,
But now she looks broken,
And her little boy, a pretty little fellow
Whom I have loved for the sake of Basil,
Looks thin and pale.
He seems scarcely at all grown
Since the first time I saw him.

೩. 20

The snow still lies upon the ground.

Just at the closing-in of the day,
I heard a cart pass the door,
And at the same time,
The dismal sound of a crying infant.
I went to the window,
And had light enough to see
That a man was driving a cart
Which seemed not to be very full,
A woman with an infant in her arms
Was following close behind,
And a dog close to her.
It was a wild and melancholy sight.

ᾶ. 21

I gathered mosses in Easedale.
I saw before me,
Sitting in the open field
Upon his pack of rags,
The old Ragman that I know.
His coat is of scarlet in a thousand patches.

≈. 22

The moon hung
Over the northern side
Of the highest point of Silver How—
Like a gold ring
Snapped in two
And shaven off at the ends.
Within this ring
There lay
The circle of the round moon
As distinctly to be seen
As ever
The enlightened moon is.

ॐ. 23

The moon was a good height
Above the mountains;
She seemed far distant in the sky.
There were two stars beside her
That twinkled in and out
And seemed almost like butterflies
In motion and lightness.
They looked to be
Far nearer to us than the moon.

🍃. 24

A sweet evening,
As it had been a sweet day,
And I walked quietly
Along the side of Rydale lake
With quiet thoughts.
The hills and the lake were still—
The owls had not begun to hoot,
And the little birds had given over singing.

🔊 25

The lake was covered all over
With bright silver waves
That were each
The twinkling of an eye.

ぁ. 26

As I climbed the moss,
The moon came out
From behind a mountain mass
Of black clouds.
O, the unutterable darkness of the sky
And the earth below the moon,
And the glorious brightness of the moon itself!

忝 27

When I saw
    this lowly building
    in the waters;
Among the dark
    and lofty hills,
With that bright
    soft light
    upon it,
It made me
    more than half
    a poet.

※. 28

The fire flutters
    and the watch ticks.
I hear nothing
    save the breathing of my Beloved.

29

Thomas Wilkinson
Came with me to Barton,
And questioned me like a catechiser
All the way.
Every question
Was like the snapping
Of a little thread about my heart.

30

I walked along the lake side.
The air was become still,
The lake was of a bright slate colour,
The hills darkening,
The bays
Shot into the low fading shores,
Sheep resting,
All things quiet.
When I returned,
William was come.
The surprise shot through me.

৯ 31

I never saw daffodils so beautiful.
They grew among the mossy stones—
About and about them;
Some rested their heads upon these stones,
As on a pillow, for weariness;
And the rest tossed and reeled and danced,
And seemed
As if they verily laughed with the wind
That blew upon them over the lake.

꩜ 32

We watched the crows,
At a little distance from us,
Become white as silver
As they flew in the sunshine;
And when they went still further
They looked like shapes of water
Passing over the green fields.

ふ 33

I saw a robin
Chasing a scarlet butterfly.

≈. 34

The dead hedge round Benson's field
Bound together at the top
By an interlacing of ash sticks,
Which made a chain of silver
When we faced the moon.

꩜. 35

Above rose the Coniston Fells
In their own shape and colour,
Not man's hills,
But all for themselves—
The sky, and the clouds,
And a few wild creatures.

H. 36

It is scarce a bower—
A little parlour only,
Not enclosed by walls,
But shaped out for a resting place
By the rocks
And the ground rising about it.
It had a sweet moss carpet.

37

It is a blessed place.

We stayed till the light of day
Was going,
And the little birds
Began to settle their singing.
But there was a thrush
That seemed to sing louder
And clearer
Than the thrushes had sung
When it was quite day.

潭. 38

Three
    solitary stars
    in the middle
    of the blue vault. ⁻ sky
One
    or two
    on the points
    of the high hills.

꩜ 39

Two ravens
Flew high, high in the sky,
And the sun shone
Upon their bellies and their wings
Long after
There was none of his light to be seen.

꩜. 40

It is a glorious wild solitude
Under that lofty purple crag.
It stood upright by itself;
Its own self and its shadow below,
One mass.
All else was sunshine.

A bird
At the top of the crag
Was flying round
And round
And looked,
In thinness
And transparency,
Shape, and motion,
Like a moth.

~ 41

O, thought I!
What a beautiful thing
God has made winter to be,
By stripping the trees,
And letting us see
Their shapes and forms.
What a freedom does it seem
To give to the storms.

ਨ. 42

The young bullfinches
In their party-coloured raiment
Bustle about
Among the blossoms
And poise themselves
Like wire-dancers or tumblers,
Shaking the twigs
And dashing off the blossoms.

43

The columbine
    is a graceful
    slender creature;
A female seeking retirement,
    and growing freest,
    and most graceful
Where it is most alone.

44

He said he had been a soldier,
That his wife and children
Had died in Jamaica.
He had a beggar's wallet over his shoulders,
And a coat of shreds and patches.
And though his body was bent,
He was tall
And had the look of one
Used to have been upright.

I talked a while, and then
I gave him a piece of cold bacon
And a penny.

ॐ 45

The swallows come
To the sitting-room window
As if wishing to build,
But I am afraid they will not have courage for it;
I believe they will build in my room window.
They twitter, and make a bustle,
And a cheerful little song,
Hanging against the panes of glass
With their soft white bellies
And their forked fish-like tails.
They swim round and round,
And again they come.

🐚 46

The shutters were closed,
But I heard the birds singing.
There was our own thrush
Shouting
With an impatient shout;
So it sounded to me.
The morning was still,
The twittering of the little birds
Was very gloomy.
The owls had hooted
A quarter of an hour before.
Now
The cocks were crowing,
It was near daylight,
I put out my candle,
And went to bed.

47

Miss Hudson of Workington called.
She said, "I sow flowers in the parks
Several miles from home, and my mother and I
Visit them, and watch them how they grow."

This may show that botanists
May be often deceived
When they find rare flowers
Growing far from houses.

48

We talked sweetly together
About the disposal of our riches.
We lay upon the sloping turf.
Earth and sky were so lovely
That they melted our very hearts.
The sky to the north
Was of a chastened yet rich yellow, fading
Into pale blue,
And streaked and scattered over
With steady islands of purple
Melting away
Into shades of pink.
It was like a vision to me.

ﬁ. 49

It is now eight o'clock;
I will go and see
If my swallows are on their nest.
Yes! there they are,
Side by side,
Both looking down into the garden.

50

O, beautiful place!
Dear Mary, William,
The hour is come.
I must prepare to go.
The swallows,
I must leave them,
The well, the garden, the roses,
All.
Dear creatures!
They sang last night
After I was in bed;
Seemed to be singing
To one another
Just before
They settled to rest.

51

Delightful walks
After the heat of the day was passed—
Seeing far off in the west
The coast of England,
Like a cloud crested
With Dover castle,
Which was but like the summit of the cloud;
The evening star
And the glory of the sky.
The reflections in the water
Were more beautiful
Than the sky itself,
Purple waves brighter
Than precious stones,
For ever melting away upon the sands.

Now came in view,
As the evening star sunk down,
And the colours of the west
Faded away,
The two lights of England,
Lighted up by Englishmen
In our country
To warn vessels off rocks or sands.

🐦 52

It was beautiful
On the calm hot night
To see the little boats
Row out of harbour
With wings of fire;
And the sail-boats
With the fiery track which they cut
As they went along,
And which closed up after them—
With a hundred thousand sparkles,
And streams of glow-worm light.

꒳. 53

Far far off from us,
In the western sky,
We saw shapes of castles,
Ruins among groves;
A great spreading wood,
Rocks
And single trees.
A minster
With its tower unusually distinct,
Minarets,
And a round Grecian Temple too.
The colours of the sky
Of a bright grey,
And the forms
Of a sober grey
With a dome.

꩜ 54

There was too much water in the river
For the beauty of the falls,
And even the banks were less interesting than in winter.
Nature had entirely got the better
In her struggles against the giants
Who first cast the mould of these works;
For indeed it is a place
That did not in winter
Remind one of God,
But one could not help feeling
As if there had been the agency
Of some "mortal instruments"
Which Nature had been struggling against
Without making a perfect conquest.
There was something so wild
And new in this feeling,
Knowing, as we did, in the inner man,
That God alone
Had laid His hand upon it,
I could not help regretting
The want of it.

55

It is a breathless, grey day,
That leaves the golden woods of autumn
Quiet in their own tranquillity,
Stately and beautiful in their decaying.

56

All things looked cheerless
And distinct;
No meltings of sky into mountains.
The mountains like stone work
Wrought up
With huge hammers.

SCOTLAND

(1803)

AND

A MOUNTAIN RAMBLE

(1805)

🔊 57

A delicious spot
In which to breathe out
A summer's day—
Limestone rocks, hanging trees,
Pools, and waterbreaks,
Caves and caldrons
Which have been honoured
With fairy names
And no doubt continue
In the fancy of the neighbourhood
To resound with fairy revels.

58

Watching the swallows
That flew about restlessly,
And flung their shadows
Upon the sunbright walls of the old building;
The shadows glanced and twinkled,
Interchanged and crossed each other,
Expanded and shrunk up,
Appeared and disappeared, every instant;
As I observed to William and Coleridge,
Seeming more like living things
Than the birds themselves.

59

The road, treeless,
Over a peat-moss common—
The Solway Moss;
Here and there an earth-built hut
With its peat stack,
A scanty-growing willow hedge
Round the kail garth,
Perhaps the cow pasturing near,
A little lass watching it—
The dreary waste cheered
By the endless singing of larks.

⁀ 60

The village of Thornhill,
Built by the Duke of Queensberry;
The "brother-houses" so small
That they might have been built
To stamp a character of insolent pride
On his own huge mansion of Drumlanrigg,
Which is full in view
On the opposite side of the Nith.

≋. 61

We saw three boys
Who came down
The cleft of a brow on our left;
One carried a fishing-rod,
And the hats of all
Were braided with honeysuckles;
They ran after one another
As wanton as the wind.

They went to school
And learned Latin, Virgil,
And one of them, Greek, Homer,
But when Coleridge began to inquire further,
Off they ran!

62

He had no hat on,
And only had a grey plaid wrapped about him.
It is nothing to describe,
But on a bare moor,
Alone with his sheep,
Standing as he did
In utter quietness
And silence. . . .

꙰ 63

The evening sun was now sending
A glorious light through the street,
Which ran from west to east.
The houses were of a fire red,
And the faces of the people,
As they walked westward,
Were almost like a blacksmith
When he is at work
By night.

৯. 64

The beauties of a brook or river
Must be sought,
And the pleasure is
In going in search of them.
Those of a lake
Or of the sea
Come to you of themselves.

ﾐ. 65

It was no more
Than a smoky vessel
Lying at anchor,
With its bare masts;
A clay hut,
And the shelving bank of the river.

66

They lived nicely with their cow:
She was meat, drink, and company.
Before breakfast
The housewife was milking
Behind the chimney,
And I thought I had seldom heard
A sweeter fire-side sound;
In an evening, sitting
Over a sleepy, low-burnt fire,
It would lull one
Like the purring of a cat.

🌊 67

Sea-birds flying
Overhead;
The noise of torrents
Mingled
With the beating of the waves,
And misty mountains
Enclosed the vale.

68

The immeasurable water,
The lofty mist-covered steeps of Morven,
The emerald islands without a bush or tree,
The celestial colour and brightness of the calm sea,
And the innumerable creeks and bays—
The communion of land and water
As far as the eye could travel.

忝. 69

A sea-hamlet,
Without trees,
Under a naked stony mountain,
Yet perfectly sheltered,
Standing in the middle of a large bay
Which half the winds
That travel over the lake
Can never visit.

70

The stars were beginning to appear,
But the brightness of the west
Was not yet gone;
The lake perfectly still,
And when we first went into the boat
We rowed almost close to the shore
Under steep crags hung with birches:
It was like a new-discovered country
Of which we had not dreamed.

We hardly spoke to each other
As we moved along receding from the west,
Which diffused a solemn animation
Over the lake.
The sky was cloudless,
And everything seemed at rest
Except our solitary boat,
And the mountain streams,
Seldom heard, and but faintly.

🎵 71

The wind was tossing their branches,
And sunshine dancing among the leaves,
And I happened to exclaim,
"What a life there is in trees!"

স্ 72

And the slim fawns
That we used to startle from their couching places
Among the fern at the top of the hill.

꙾ 73

As we went along
The mist gathered upon the valleys,
And it even rained
All the way to the head of Patterdale;
But there was never a drop upon my habit larger
Than the smallest pearls upon a lady's ring.

☙ 74

The rocky shore,
Spotted and streaked
With purplish brown heath,
And its image in the water, together
Were like an immense caterpillar.

THE CONTINENT

(1820)

꩜ 75

I remembered
The shapeless wishes of my youth—
Wishes without hope—
My brother's wanderings thirty years ago,
And the tales brought to me
The following Christmas holidays at Forncett,
And often repeated
While we paced together
On the gravel walk in the parsonage garden,
By moon or star light.

🔊 76

I saw the snows of the Alps
Burnished by the sun
About half an hour before his setting.
After that
They were left to their wintry marble coldness,
Without a farewell gleam.
Yet suddenly the city
And the cathedral tower and trees
Were singled out for favor by the sun
Among his glittering clouds,
And gilded with the richest light.
A few minutes, and that glory vanished.

🔊 77

On our right was the Jungfrau
In stillness of deepest winter;
And the opposite hill, the Wengern,
Was carpeted with green grass and flowers.

〜. 78

All night,
And all day,
And for ever,
The vale of Meiringen
Is sounding with torrents.

శ. 79

The river Po,
A ghostly serpent-line,
Rested on the brown plains of Lombardy.

ॐ 80

Skeletons of tall pine-trees
Beneath us in the dell,
And above our heads—
Their stems and shattered branches
As grey
As the stream of the Vedra,
Or the crags
Strewn at their feet.

శ. 8 1

A small plot or two of turf,
Never to be cropped by goat or heifer,
On the ledge of a precipice;
A bunch of slender flowers
Hanging from a chink;
And one luxuriant plot
Of bright blue monkshood,
Lodged like a little garden
Amid the stone-work of an Italian villa,
Were the sole marks of vegetation,
Except a few distorted pine trees on one of the summits,
Which reminded us of watchmen
On the look-out.

SCOTLAND
(1 8 2 2)
AND
THE ISLE OF MAN
(1 8 2 8)

忝. 8 2

No sound
But of the robins
Continually singing.
Sometimes
A distant oar on the waters,
And now and then
Reapers at work
Above
On the hills.

漁. 83

The moon
Rose large and dull,
Like an ill-cleaned brass plate;
Slowly surmounts the haze
And sends
Over the calm sea
A faint bright pillar.

ॡ 84

Douglas harbour illuminated;
Boats in motion,
Dark masts and eloquent ropes;
Noises from the town
Ascend
To the commanding airy steeps.